MAD'S®

CRADLE TO GRAVE PRIMER

Written by **LARRY SIEGEL**
Illustrated by **GEORGE WOODBRIDGE**

Edited by Nick Meglin

D1247485

WARNER BOOKS

A Warner Communications Company

WARNER BOOKS EDITION

ISBN: 0-446-88906-7

This Warner Books Edition is published by
arrangement with E.C. Publications, Inc.

Warner Books, Inc., 75 Rockefeller Plaza, New York, N.Y. 10019

Ⓦ A Warner Communications Company

Printed in the United States of America

Not associated with Warner Press, Inc. of Anderson, Indiana

First Printing: June, 1973

Reissued: June, 1979

10   9   8   7   6

CHAPTER 1

INFANCY

See the baby.
What a nice baby.
It is YOU!
You are less than a minute old.
See the doctor hold you.
Soon he will give you a stinging slap on the rump.
You will scream your fool head off.
You don't know it yet
But this will be the nicest thing to happen to you
For the rest of your life.
From here on in, it is all downhill.
You are a born loser!

Who is this nice lady?
She is your mother.
See how she smiles at you.
She loves you.
Perhaps she will always love you.
Perhaps she will love you very much.
Perhaps she will love you very, very much.
Perhaps she will love you too much.
How will you know?
If, when you are 16,
You go to the beach
And borrow her bikini.

Who is that man?
He is your father.
He thinks you are strange-looking.
He thinks you look ratty.
He will probably ignore you
Until you are better looking.
Take a good look at him.
You may never see him again.

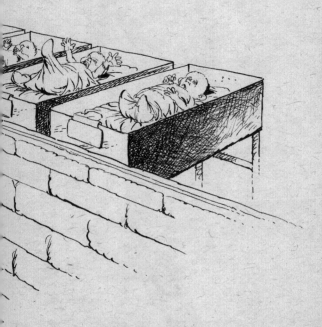

Look, your Daddy is waving goodbye.
Wave bye-bye at Da-Da.
Ha ha ha.
I forgot.
You can't wave yet.
You are too young.
All you can do is cry
And throw up.
Now that Daddy has seen you,
What will he do?
Probably cry
And throw up.

Isn't it nice to be home?
Who is that little girl?
She is your sister.
She didn't want you very much.
She expected a dog.
She wanted someone to fetch for her,
To obey her commands,
To sit up and beg,
To tie up with a rope to a tree.
You don't know it yet,
But you're going to be a dog.

See the odd creatures staring at you.
Who are they?
They are your relatives.
"Ga ga ga," says one.
"Goo goo goo," says another.
"Cluck cluck cluck," says a third.
They have come a long way to see you.
Where have they come from?
Probably from a barnyard.
You may not speak your first word of English
For years.
That's because you may not *hear* your first word
Of English
For years.

You are one month old now.
You are miserable.
You are crying.
Here comes Da-Da.
He has come to take care of you.
Why has he come to take care of you?
For the same reason all devoted, loving fathers
Take care of babies
Who are wet
And hungry
And dirty
At 3 in the morning.
Mommy makes them.

What a nice Da-Da he is.
He would like to soothe you
And feed you
And change you
And kill you.
Not necessarily in that order.
You will always remember this moment
Between now
And your first visit to your psychiatrist.

You have your first tooth.
How proud your Mommy is.
It is a big moment.
The whole family is happy.
Your sister isn't happy.
Why isn't she happy?
Because Mommy is holding you and not her.
She is jealous.
Soon Mommy will leave the room.
Wave bye-bye to Mommy.
Soon sister will punch you in the mouth.
Wave bye-bye to your first tooth.

My, my, how you've grown.
Now you are crawling all over the house.
You are so curious.
You put everything in your mouth.
What funny things you eat.
Like paper and ants
And glass and nails
And dirt.
Mommy is worried about you.
She thinks you may choke to death.
Do not worry, Mommy.
Look at it this way.
You're not losing a son.
You're gaining a vacuum cleaner.

What a big day today is.
Today you said your first word.
Why did you get clobbered?
Because you said the wrong word.
You used a word you heard Daddy call Mommy.
Only he didn't call her "Mommy."
"Mommy" has five letters.
His word had four.
How could you know the difference?
Actually you couldn't.
This is what is known as grown-up justice.
You will learn more about it in later years.
During your *second* visit to your psychiatrist.

Hurray for the baby.
You are taking your very first steps.
Then you fall down on your face.
Then you get up and take another step.
Then you fall on your face again.
Poor baby.
You want to walk just like Daddy?
Where is Daddy now?
He is at a grown-up party. . .
Getting bombed.
We have news for you.
Right now you *are* walking like Daddy.

Who is that little girl?
She is your first playmate.
Her name is Nancy.
She is a born winner.
She hits you on the head.
She takes your pail.
She takes your shovel,
She takes your toys.
She takes you for everything you've got.
With her luck,
You will probably be blamed for everything.
With your luck,
You will probably marry her.

Look at you now.
You met a doctor who belted you.
You met your parents who don't understand you.
You met a sister who hates you.
You had a tooth that was knocked out.
You ate poison in the kitchen.
And you almost broke your head trying to walk.
Wasn't infancy fun?
You will never forget it.
Even if you live to be three.

CHAPTER 2

CHILDHOOD

You are three years old.
What a big boy you are.
Look at Mommy clapping her hands.
She is so happy.
Why is she happy?
Because you have gone all by yourself
For the very first time.
She is very proud of you.
Mommies are very sentimental.
They save locks of your hair.
They bronze your baby shoes.
They bronze *everything*.
Soon she will look in your potty.
Will she or won't she?
Only her bronzer will know for sure.

You are crying.
I know why you are crying.
Remember how Mommy saw you sit on your potty
And she clapped her hands?
Well you walked in and saw Mommy sit on *her* potty.
And you clapped *your* hands.
Then Mommy clapped her hands again.
But this time your head was between them.
This is another sample of grown-up justice.
Doesn't life get better all the time?

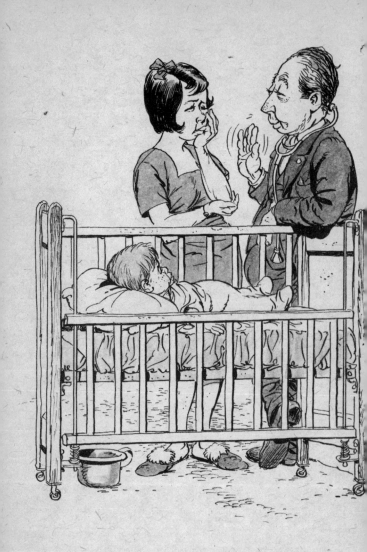

Here is your sister again.
For years she has been taking your toys
And your books
And your balls
And your games.
Well now she has decided to *give* you something
For a change.
She is sweet, after all.
What did she decide to give you?
The chicken pox.

Aren't childhood diseases fun?
They never seem to end.
Don't worry.
Some day they will be all over.
And you will be up and around
And you will feel fine
And your face will be all clear again.
As you grow older,
It is important for your face to be clear
Of chicken pox and measles and mumps.
You will need the room for acne.

What an active boy you are now.
You build houses with blocks.
You scribble on paper.
You break toys.
And you are painting all over the room
With your fingers.
Isn't it fun to do things with your fingers?
Look at Mommy.
She wants to do things with her fingers too.
Like wrap them around your rotten neck.

Mommy has sent you to nursery school.
What are they teaching you in nursery school?
How to build houses with blocks.
How to scribble on paper.
How to break toys.
And how to paint all over the room
With your fingers.
Isn't education wonderful?

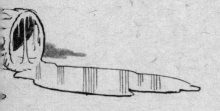

You have been in nursery school for three months now.
What have you learned there?
Nothing.
What has Mommy learned?
Plenty.
Namely, the best way to get rid of a rotten kid
Is to send him to nursery school.
Isn't it great to feel wanted?
The next time you go to the post office,
You will see the pictures of ten men on the wall.
They feel wanted too.

Now you are old enough to go to regular school.
Isn't it nice to be with children your own age?
Bright, eager youngsters
With but one thought on their minds.
To make life as miserable as possible for you.
They hit you,
They spit on you,
They tear your books.
They call you, "Four-eyes."
"Four-eyes" is a terrible thing to call
A sensitive child like you.
Particularly when you don't even wear glasses.

Now you wear glasses.
You also wear braces.
And you are a head shorter than the other kids.
Boy, are you a mess.
The kids still pick on you.
But you won't stand for it anymore.
You'll tell them a thing or two.
You'll tell them your eyes will get better.
You'll tell them your teeth will be straight.
You'll tell them you'll grow tall.
You'll tell them a lot of things.
As soon as you stop stuttering.

Isn't this nice?
You are playing Little League baseball.
What is going on here?
Your father is arguing with the umpire.
Fathers always argue during Little League games.
They take the game much more seriously than their sons do.
Doesn't it make you feel secure to know
That your father is so interested in your game?
Wouldn't you feel a lot more secure
If you knew your father were arguing *for* you
Instead of *against* you?

Who is this pretty little girl?
She is your neighbor.
Isn't she sweet?
She would like to play Doctor with you.
"I will be the patient," she says.
"I will take off my clothes."
"Then what will you do?" she asks.
"I will be the doctor," you say.
"I will tell you to put your clothes back on
Or else you will catch a bad cold."
Perhaps you'd better stick to baseball.

Who are these ugly people?
They are your aunt and uncle.
They have come to visit you.
They will tell you how much you've grown.
They will tell you how good looking you are.
They will tell you what a nice boy you are.
They will tell you other lies.
Soon they will be leaving.
Thank God.
Soon they will kiss you goodbye.
Soon you will feel a sharp, bristling moustache
Scraping your face.
After that your *uncle* will kiss you.

The BLITZ BUTCHERS
AND
SGT. SUICIDE

You are nine years old now.
Your family is going to a movie.
"What movie would you like to see?" they ask you.
"I would like to see a sex movie," you tell them.
"Why a sex movie?" your parents say, horrified.
"Perhaps I can learn the facts of life," you say.
"You will not see a sex movie," say your parents.
"They are dirty.
They are not for children.
We will see a nice war movie instead."
According to grown-up logic,
Love-making is bad for children.
But killing is good.
But all is not lost after all.
You have already learned *one* fact of life.

You are going to summer camp.
Won't you have fun?
Probably not.
But you are going anyway.
Why are you going?
Because your parents want to get rid of you,
And you are too old to go to nursery school.
It is your first sleepaway.
You are lucky.
Your father didn't go to his first sleepaway
Until he was 37.
But that wasn't a camp.
And your mother almost killed him.
But that's another story.

Isn't camp fun?
Not really.
You have lost half your clothes.
You have been sick 12 times.
And you've been bitten 100 times
By mosquitoes, wasps
And a midget camper.
All your bunk-mates have gotten merit badges.
For swimming,
For arts and crafts,
And for archery.
Will you get a special award too?
You deserve one.
How many other campers have ever caught poison ivy
On the bus ride to camp?

Congratulations.
You have just made it through childhood.
And you are still in one piece.
More or less.
You have struggled through toilet training.
You have suffered through childhood diseases.
You have staggered through elementary school.
And you were almost destroyed in camp.
But look at it this way:
Things can't get any worse.
On second thought, they *can* get worse.
You are now a teenager.

CHAPTER 3

ADOLESCENCE

Hi there, teenager.
What are you doing on the street corner?
This is where you will learn about sex.
Most teenagers already *know* about sex.
They know about it by the time they arrive at Puberty.
You haven't arrived at Puberty yet.
You have enough trouble finding your way
Home from school.

One of the boys is telling the facts of life.
He is telling them all wrong.
What he says is disgusting.
You get sick and throw up.
Wait, there is another boy.
He is a smart boy.
He is very experienced.
Now *he* is telling the facts of life.
He is telling them right.
He is telling it like it is.
You get sick and throw up again.

You are going through a difficult period now.
You are very ungainly.
Your feet are like sticks.
Your arms are like toothpicks.
Your posture is terrible.
Your voice is changing.
And you have acne.
All over your body.
But you can't lose heart.
All this will change.
You will outgrow this.
Before you know it,
You will go into the awkward age.

You hang around the house a lot.
You usually flop in corners.
You hardly speak.
You seldom move.
You barely breathe.
Once a day your father takes your pulse.
Once a week your mother dusts you.
On weekends your parents throw a cloth over you
And eat dinner on your back.
It's the closest you've been to them in years.

This is the age of the generation gap.
This is the age when teenagers
Show their independence.
This is when they pack their things
And run away from home.
See your parents cry.
You are breaking their hearts.
Why are you so unreasonable?
Why do you treat them like this?
Why don't you make them happy again?
Why don't you run away from home
Like everyone else?

This is your high school friend.
His name is Bruce.
He is not like you at all.
He is very sure of himself.
He is a swinger.
He can get any girl he wants.
You admire his looks.
You envy his personality.
You like his confidence.
You hate his guts.

You are going on your first date.
It is a girl Bruce fixed you up with.
He couldn't stand her.
She was always pawing at him
And kissing him
And biting his ear.
She is overbearing,
And overwrought,
And oversexed.
She was a problem to him.
You should have such problems.

This is your date's house.
You are very nervous.
You have but one thing on your mind,
As you think about your date.
It is the only thing you thought of
When you left your house.
It is the only thing you thought of
On the bus.
It is the only thing you think of now
As you wait for her.
Where's the nearest bathroom?

This is your date.
This is the girl Bruce couldn't stand.
Because she was always pawing at him
And kissing him
And biting his ear.
This is the girl who is overbearing,
And overwrought,
And oversexed,
And over there.
If she is so oversexed,
Why are you over here
While she is over there?

Three hours have passed.
You haven't said a word
Or moved a muscle.
What are you waiting for?
Why don't you start something?
There are three reasons
Why you don't start anything.
You don't know how to start,
You don't know where to start,
And you don't know *what* to start.
Aside from this,
You have everything under control.
Isn't dating fun?

Now you have started.
Oh boy, have you ever started.
All your built-up passion,
All your desire,
Everything you have been holding back
For all these years
Has now come out.
In one wild, mad, smouldering kiss.
"What a lover I have suddenly become," you think.
"No girl can resist me now.
From here on in it's one conquest after another.
Look at how she melts in my arms.
Listen to those strange animal noises she is making.
I wonder what they mean."
This is what they mean.
They are not animal noises.
She is just having trouble yawning
With her mouth closed.

What a kiss that was.
She must be wild about you.
You could go for a girl like her.
She is not like the other girls you have met.
She is not silly.
She is not frivolous.
She takes you seriously.
Very, very seriously.
How can you tell?
When you asked her
If she'd like to go steady with you,
She said, "Don't make me laugh."

You are 18 years old now.
High school was rough.
You had nothing in common with any of
The other students.
Now you are in college.
You study hard.
You don't smoke pot.
You don't demonstrate.
You don't live off-campus with girls.
You have nothing in common
With anyone here either.

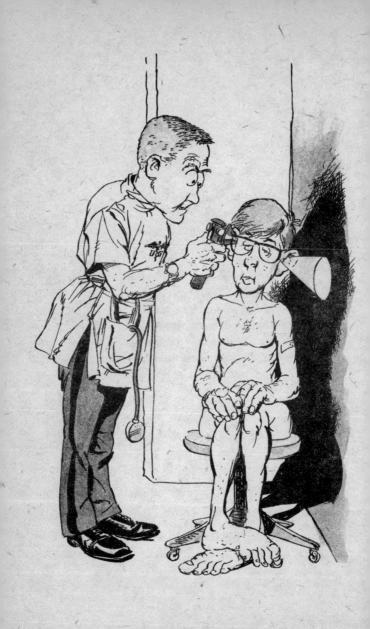

Where are you now?
This is a draft board.
You are being tested to see if you are fit
To serve your country.
There are several reasons why many young men
Are turned down for the service.
Some are turned down for medical reasons.
Others for mental reasons.
Others because they wear mascara.
You are the only American in history
Who may be excused from military service
For being a Conscientious Nebbish.

You are 21 years old.
You are graduating from college.
Are you ready now for manhood?
Are you ready to get a job?
To get married?
To raise a family?
To fight for the freedom of your fellow man?
Regardless of race, color, or creed?
No.
No.
No.
No.
No.
No no no.

CHAPTER 4

ADULTHOOD

Look at you now.
You have come a long way.
Look at that face.
Look at that build.
Look at that posture.
Isn't it exciting?
You are no longer
A skinny, ugly, awkward kid.
You are now
A skinny, ugly, awkward *adult*.

You still hang around the house.
You still don't do much.
But something new has happened.
Your parents no longer ignore you.
Now they are aware of you.
Now they speak to you.
They say things to you like,
"Why don't you get the hell out of the house?
Why don't you find a girl and settle down?
Why don't you find a *boy* and settle down?"
This is a terrible thing to say.
It can make a young man doubt his masculinity.
You'll see.
One of these days you'll find your masculinity.
Then, boy, will you doubt it!

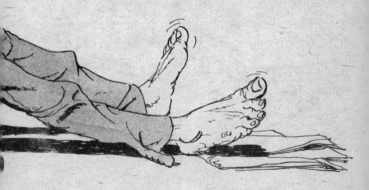

Well, you have finally made the big break.
You have moved out of your house.
All your friends are independent.
Now you are independent.
All your friends have their own pads.
Now you have yours.
All your friends have soft, warm companions
Who share their beds and blow in their ears.
Now you can get yourself a dog.

You have just got your first job.
You are an accountant.
Accountants work day and night over dull ledgers.
They tell dull stories.
They wear grey suits.
They carry 14 ball point pens
In their jacket pockets.
They read books like,
"The Romance of the W-2 Form."
Accountants are the most boring people in the world.
How do you fit in here?
Let me put it this way?
Other accountants will find *you* dull.

This is a psychiatrist.
He tries to help you with your problems.
You ask him questions,
He answers your questions
With other questions.
You ask, "Why do girls ignore me?"
He says, "Why do you think girls ignore you?"
You ask, "What's wrong with me?"
He says, "What do you think is wrong with you?"
You ask, "What should I do?"
He says, "What do you want to do?"
You ask, "How much do I owe you?"
He says, "Fifty dollars."
There is no question about *that*.

Where are you now?
This is a group therapy session.
Here is how group therapy works.
You don't lie on a couch
And tell your problems to a psychiatrist,
And then pay the psychiatrist.
Instead you sit in a chair
And tell your problems to nine strangers
And then pay the psychiatrist.
It has been proved that group therapy
Is ten times better than individual therapy.
Not necessarily for you.
For the psychiatrist.

You are really moving right along.
What are you doing now?
This is an encounter group.
It is supposed to help you release your blocked emotions.
People walk around the room kissing each other
And touching each other
And feeling each other.
It works wonders for patients.
Some people lose their frustrations.
Other people lose their inhibitions.
The only thing you have lost so far
Is your wallet.

Who is this girl?
Her name is Blanche.
You met her at an Accountants' Masquerade Ball.
She came dressed as a debit column
In a ledger.
Take a good look at her.
You will be seeing a lot of her.
She is the girl of your dreams.
No wonder you haven't had a good night's sleep
For the past 25 years.

Here are Blanche's parents.
They are very religious people.
When you said you would like to marry their daughter,
They both said, "Thank God!"
They are very happy.
They have consented to give you
Their daughter's hand in marriage.
There is just one problem.
You will have to take the rest that goes with it.

This is your wedding day.
Isn't it thrilling?
Look at everyone cry.
Everyone always cries at weddings.
Look at you,
Standing next to the woman
Who will always be by your side
And live with you
And share your bed
For the rest of your life.
Is that why *you* are crying?

You and Blanche are finally married.
Boy, are you nervous.
You almost lost the plane tickets.
You got the hotel rooms mixed up.
And you dropped your bride
While carrying her across the threshold.
Some wedding night!
Can *anything* else possibly go wrong?
Yes.

You have been married for a year now.
Here are the things you own
Which you can't afford:
A washing machine,
A dryer,
A TV set,
A car,
And a wife.
The finance company will be here soon
To take back their things.
No sign of Blanche's parents yet.

Look at your wife.
Notice how round she has become.
See how her belly protrudes.
Do you know what that means?
Of course you do.
It means she is eating for two.
In other words, she is pregnant?
No, in other words, she is a pig.

Now she is pregnant.
Boy, is she ever pregnant.
She drives you crazy.
She wakes you up in the middle of the night.
She asks for pickles smothered in peanut butter
And cucumbers and buttermilk
And asparagus dipped in chicken fat.
But you take it all in stride.
After all, this is what she ate
Before she was pregnant.

This is a waiting room.
You are waiting for your new baby.
You smoke nervously and pace the floor.
Look at the other expectant father.
The doctor told him his wife might have triplets
Or maybe quadruplets
Or even quintuplets.
How come he's not nervous too?
I don't think he is smoking
What *you* are smoking.

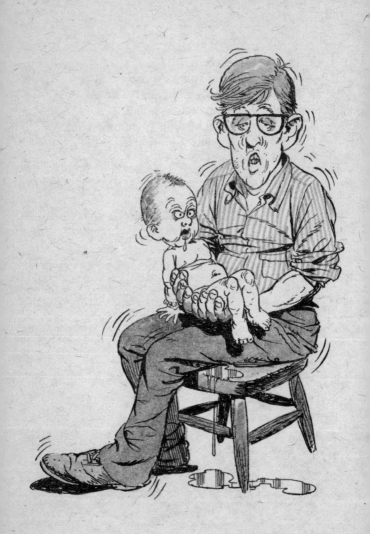

Congratulations.
You are now a father.
This is your new baby.
But he is more than just a baby.
He is life itself.
And you have helped bring forth this new life.
See how he comforts you.
See how he thrills you.
See how he does things all over you.
Why are you so surprised?
Isn't that what life has been doing to you
For the past 30 years?

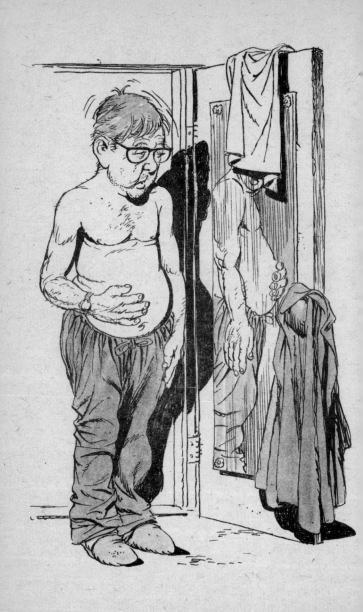

CHAPTER 5

MIDDLE AGE

You are 40.
You have reached middle age.
It is a tricky period in life.
It is a time when most people are concerned
About their health
And their weight
And their appearance.
It's the age when everyone is worried about going
Downhill.
How come *you're* not worried about going downhill?
Perhaps it's because
For *you* it's not much of a drop.

Who are these two children?
They are your son and your daughter.
He is 10 and she is 7.
They are so self-assured.
My, how times change.
When you were that age,
You weren't a bone-crunching fullback
In the Little Leagues.
You couldn't beat up every kid
On the block.
You didn't use words that would embarrass
A truck-driver.
To think a kid of yours would be doing all that.
And what's more, your son is pretty tough too.

See your son and daughter.
They are fighting.
They always fight.
When they are not fighting,
They are messing.
Tonight is a big night.
They are fighting and messing.
Look at the condition of your house.
It has looked like this for as long
As you can remember.
You try to remember the last time
The house looked neater.
Then you recall.
It was on Wednesday last July,
The night you were robbed.

Now you are 45.
Now you worry about everything.
You are particularly worried about your health.
When you cough you think you have TB.
When your leg hurts you think you have arthritis.
When you eat cake you think you have diabetes.
But you don't worry about TB
And arthritis
And diabetes
All the time.
There are days when the sun is shining
And the birds are singing
And the flowers are blooming
And the world is smiling.
That's when you worry about cancer.

The doctor tells you
It is good to worry about cancer.
Because if you worry about cancer
You have frequent check-ups
And you can stop it in its early stages.
He is checking you now.
He tells you that you don't have cancer.
Don't you feel better now?
And aren't you glad you worried about it?
No, you definitely don't have cancer.
But you do have something else.
What do you have?
You have ulcers and heart trouble.
How do you think you got ulcers and heart trouble?
Probably from worrying about cancer?

You are very diet conscious.
You ask your doctor what to eat.
He tells you to go on a high protein diet.
So you cut out cake and milk and butter
And you eat eggs and sea food.
Now your doctor tells you your fat content is down
But your cholesterol is up.
So you cut out eggs and sea food
And you eat cheese.
Now your doctor tells you your fat content is down
And your cholesterol is down,
But your triglicerides are up.
So you stop eating *all* food.
You decide to drink nothing but water.
Can water hurt you?
Don't ask your doctor.
Ask a swordfish.

What are you doing now?
You are jogging.
Many middle-aged men jog.
What happens when you jog?
The soles of your feet get hot.
The backs of your ankles get sore.
Your thighs are like raw meat.
You gasp and wheeze,
You choke and gag,
You cough and spit,
You throw up and collapse.
If it does all that to you,
How come you jog?
Because it feels so good when you stop.
Ha ha ha, you say.
That's an old joke.
Ha ha ha, I say.
So are you.

Look at your son now.
He is a groovy teenager.
He is not at all like you
When you were his age.
He drives a hot rod.
He surfs.
He swings with every girl in town.
When you were his age
You were just beginning to *think* about sex.
He's thinking of *retiring*.
Undefeated.

Look at your son and his girl.
Isn't he a bum?
Why isn't he out working?
Why isn't he doing something worthwhile?
These kids nowadays!
Listen to that horrible music.
There's no peace with them around the house.
How you wish he'd leave the room.
How you wish he'd leave the house.
How you wish he'd leave the girl.
Right where she is.

You have trouble sleeping.
You keep thinking about your son.
Even worse,
You keep thinking about his girl.
How could you and your son be so different?
It doesn't figure.
Wait a minute.
Maybe he's *not* your son.
Maybe early in your marriage
Your wife had a lover.
Someone who was insane about her
And carried her off to a moonlit shore
And made mad, passionate love to her.
You turn.
You take a good, long look at your wife.
No, he's your son.

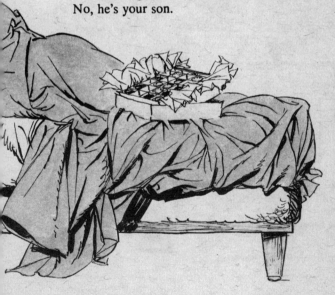

You are very depressed.
You go to the doctor.
He says, what is wrong with you
Is not uncommon
With men your age.
You are going through a
Change of life.
Suddenly you become very happy.
You begin to giggle.
You start to dance around the room.
He says, "Why are you so happy
When I tell you, you are going through a
Change of life?"
You are suddenly depressed again.
You say, "Did you say
Change of life?
I thought you said
Change of *wife*."

Look at your daughter now.
She is 16.
She whines a lot.
She has a nasty temper.
She claims she has nothing to wear.
She never cleans her room.
She hasn't shown you one ounce of affection
For 16 years.
She is not like you at all either.
But she's a lot like her mother.

Your son and daughter are going on dates.
You know who your son is going with.
You know what he's going to do.
How you envy him.
His zest for life.
His lack of inhibitions.
In a way you're proud of him.
Perhaps this is where the future strength
Of American lies.
Freedom of thought.
Freedom of expression.
Freedom of body.
Who is your daughter going with?
You don't know.
But if it's anyone like your son,
You'll kill her.

You are now in your fifties.
You are more worried about things than ever.
You are losing your hair.
You are losing your teeth.
You need something to bolster your confidence.
You decide to have an affair.
You may also be losing your mind.

This is your secretary.
You have taken her to a motel.
She is very young.
She is very beautiful.
She is really built.
Is she too much for you?
Do you think you can handle her?
Look at it this way.
You are the New York Mets
And she is the Baltimore Orioles.
In other words you are going to score
A brilliant upset victory?
No, in other words you are
Not in her league.

Three hours have passed.
You haven't done anything.
Remember how many years ago
When you were a teenager,
You were in a similar situation with a girl?
You didn't know how to start,
You didn't know where to start,
And you didn't know *what* to start?
Well now you know how to start,
And you know where to start,
And you know *what* to start.
Well then, what's the trouble?
I don't know.
Perhaps it's with your starter.

You have just received good news from your son.
He is about to become a father.
Which means you are about to become a grandfather.
You are proud of your son.
You never dreamed that this wild, swinging kid
Would finally settle down
And do what normal people do
And have a child of his own.
Now if he'd only get married.

This is your new grandchild.
Look at him.
He is ugly.
He has no hair.
He has no teeth.
He is totally miserable.
At last,
After all these years
There is someone in the family
Who has something in common
With *you*.

CHAPTER 6

OLD AGE

Look at you now.
You have even less hair
And even more belly.
Your bones are getting soft
And your arteries are getting hard.
You are now a sexagenarian.
Isn't that a funny word?
It means you are in your sixties.
It has nothing to do with sex.
Come to think of it,
From here on in,
Neither will you.

As you grow older
You get more religious.
You begin to spend a lot more time in church.
You join the congregation in prayer.
You join them in responsive reading.
What is responsive reading?
It is where one person in church says something
And then the others say something else.
Here is an example of responsive reading
In your church.
One person says, "Bingo!"
And the others say, "Oh my God!"

In the old days when you opened your morning paper
The first thing you read was the sports section.
Now the first thing you read is the obituary column.
You are very conscious of death.
Many of your friends are gone,
Many of your relatives are gone.
Even your wife is gone.
She's not dead.
She's just gone.
She ran off with your best friend.
Actually he wasn't your best friend.
Until he ran off with your wife.

You are now 75.
You have been with your firm for 50 years.
They throw a dinner in your honor.
They make speeches about you.
Your boss gives you a gold watch.
You are thrilled.
You are touched.
You are fired.
Why were you fired?
The boss tells you he needs new blood.
You tell him you could use some new blood yourself.
You laugh.
He doesn't.
Somehow the joke doesn't work.
Somehow neither does the watch.

You have lots of time on your hands now.
You spend most of your days in the park.
The park has changed over the years.
It used to be filled with young people.
Now, thanks to medical science
And miracle drugs,
People live a lot longer.
Now the park is filled with old people.
You play shuffleboard with a
70-year-old shuffleboard player.
You play checkers with an 80-year-old checker player.
You play cards with a 90-year-old poker player.
Then you give your wallet to a 20-year-old mugger.
And you go home.
Actually the park hasn't changed *that* much.

You are now too old to take care of yourself.
Luckily you have two devoted children.
You can either stay with your son's family
Or with your daughter's family.
They have a big argument over who gets you.
They decide to toss a coin.
Your daughter wins.
You get to stay with your son.

You are now living with your son and his wife.
They take care of you.
Your legs hurt,
Your arms hurt,
Your back hurts,
Your shoulders hurt,
Your chest hurts,
Your tooth hurts.
You are just one big, massive pain
All over your body.
To them you are just one big, massive pain
In the neck.

You are now in your nineties.
Your children still love you very much.
They love you so much
They have decided to send you away for
A summer vacation.
Also a winter vacation, a spring vacation
And a fall vacation.
To an old age home.
What a lovely vacation.
An old age home is a lot like a resort hotel.
It has nice airy rooms.
It has a nice big lobby.
It has a dining room.
But there is one big difference.
At check-out time in a hotel,
You pack your things and you carry them out.
At check-out time here,
They pack your things and carry *you* out.

There is not a wasted minute
In an old age home.
The entire day is filled with planned activities.
Here is the daily schedule.
From 9:00 to 11:00 is Beginner's Rocking.
From 11:00 to 1:00 is Preliminary Complaining.
From 1:00 to 3:00 is Basic Moaning.
From 3:00 to 5:00 is Intermediate Sighing
And Chest Thumping.
From 5:00 o'clock on is Advanced Kvetching.
Isn't this a fun crowd?
When you first got to the home
You were afraid you were going to die.
Now that you have been here a month,
You are afraid you won't.

Who are all these people?
They are your children.
And their children.
And your children's children.
This is your whole family.
They have all come to visit you,
Here at the old age home,
For the first time.
What respect.
What love.
What devotion.
What *guilt*.

Why are they here?
It is your 100th birthday.
They are throwing you a surprise party.
You are in the other room.
You don't know they are here.
You don't know about the party.
Your family is so proud of you.
You have lived through every disease,
Every ailment,
Every infirmity.
You are indestructible.
Here you come now.
They quickly throw on the lights.
They all scream, "Surprise!"

That did it!

What a lovely funeral.
See your grieving family.
Listen to them open up their hearts.
"He was never sick a day in his life," says one.
Actually you had every disease under the sun.
"We'll never forget him," says another.
Half of them don't even know your name.
"Struck down in the prime of his life," says another.
You were 100 years old.
"He had so much to live for," says another.
Actually you had nothing.
"He's dead and now they're going to bury him!"
Cries another.
Well, one out of five ain't bad.

It's all over now.
A hundred years of misery.
A hundred years of aggravation.
A hundred years of frustration.
The final chapter is finished.
The curtain is down
On the miserable,
Aggravating,
Frustrating life
Of a born loser.

See the angel.
What a nice angel.
It is YOU!
You are less than a minute old in heaven.
You are smaller than the other angels.
Your wings are shabby.
Your halo is crooked.
See them laugh at you.
See them mock you.
See the bully angel.
Soon he will punch you in the mouth.
You will scream your fool head off.
You don't know it yet,
But that will be the nicest thing to happen to you
For the rest of eternity.
From here on in, it is all down-hill.
You are a dead loser!